Listen to the Whisper

Listen to the Whisper

Freedom in the Midst of the Storm

Sandi Matts

Interior Design: 11-Eleven Electronic Publishing Services

Author website - www.sandimatts.com

Acknowledgements

First and foremost, I wish to thank those who provided inspiration for the stories presented in *Listen to the Whisper*. I am the person I am today because of you.

A special thanks to John, Sharon, Ginny, Linda, Deb and my Mom who encouraged me, with each chapter, to continue the writing process. Your kind words are indelibly written on my heart. You helped me believe in myself.

I am forever grateful for Margaret, Joanne and Char who conscientiously offered their editing skills. Thank you for making me look good, I could not have done this without you. I love you more than you know.

Melinda, I cannot thank you enough for stepping in at the last moment and for your patience with all my questions. I appreciate your expertise with publishing and formatting the final design of *Listen to the Whisper*.

Above all, I give thanks to a gracious and loving God from whom all things are possible and for the countless blessings in my life, especially the gift of family and friends.

In loving memory of my Dad, who taught me to love life, to laugh, and to dance with wild abandon.

For my Mom and John, who have so faithfully supported all my new beginnings with encouragement and love.

To Jeff, Kelly, Brody, Abigail and Addison; May you always find God and purpose in those He so lovingly places on your pathway.

I love you all. I am so very blessed.

Table of Contents

Introduction

Life is a gift. The people who are part of our lives are also precious gifts. *Listen to the Whisper* offers a glimpse into not only the day-to-day experiences but also the people who have enriched my journey. My life reflects that of a common, ordinary, everyday person. I am confident readers will relate to the personal stories shared and be inspired to recognize the whisper in their own lives.

Our journeys are interwoven through the ups and downs of life, each event presented for a purpose. Daily, we are confronted by choices as countless emotions signal us to uncover the possibilities which move us forward. I've learned that love is the <u>source</u> of power on my journey; love of self, love of others and love of a higher power.

The stories which create the chapters of *Listen to the Whisper* come from the pathways I've followed and the people I've encountered along the way. In quiet reflective moments, I recognize that each experience and companion on my voyage has graced me with an abundance of knowledge and a deeper understanding of love.

I have discovered that God speaks to us through others, offering hope as we listen for the whisper. Listening for the whisper means hearing the very breath of God speaking ever so softly but confidently, through each experience of our lifetime, through each voice we hear. The whisper comes when we least expect it. We just need to be sensitive and aware.

It may be easy to recognize the whisper in the happy times, but what about through the storms? Sometimes our lives are best illustrated by a thunderstorm with wind, rain, and fear motivating our reactions. Thunderstorms are powerful. They are a metaphor for the trials of life. If we just ride out the fury, we find a rainbow on the other side with its beautiful colors offering us hope, peace, tranquility, and a greater appreciation for sunny days. It may take work to clean up after the storm, but I have learned many hands make light work. If we look, we will find a crew on stand-by willing to lend a hand.

As I seek to know and understand the essence of God who created this amazing universe and all life which dwells here, I find love and peace in the midst of this chaotic world in which we live.

Listen to the Whisper was written to help others identify and connect with their inner spirituality and to find balance. As we seek, we will find the love of God in the most unlikely places; with someone who is dying, in a prison, while running a race or sitting under a willow tree. Learning to recognize God's voice in the midst of one of life's storms will help us live a life filled with peace, joy, and happiness. As we experience these emotions, we are reminded that Love is the Source that transforms our heart and soul.

Chapter One - Dad's Story

In the midst of gasping for each breath, suffocating in pain, his eyes intensely revealed his soul, and an eagerness to go home. His eyes traveled upward to a world beyond ours...to a place beyond beauty...a place surpassing faith and hope...a universe above our mortal comprehension of love.

My mom, my brother, and I had been taking turns for days, keeping an around-the-clock vigil with Dad. The cancer had taken its toll. He fought for so long. The doctors gave him three to six months; his battle and his victory came to an end after three years.

Two nights after Christmas, I clearly remember being awakened just after 2:00 a.m. Dad's breathing had changed. Mom and I sat by his side. We held his hands, Mom on one side, me on the other. All these years later if I just close my eyes and go back in time, I can feel the warmth of his hand in mine. Dad was our rock. Sixty-six was much too young to die. We had so many plans, so much life yet to be lived. How would we go on without him?

We sat immersed in our thoughts and time, waiting and hoping for a sign – any sign of life – when we were suddenly summoned back to the present moment. Not by Dad's shallow breathing or his crying out in pain, but by a presence, an awareness of a connection to a world beyond ours. Dad's eyes opened and took on an almost hypnotic stare as they traveled across the ceiling, glazing intensely into a universe beyond our mortal comprehension. As we looked into Dad's eyes, Mom and I both understood, his time had come.

We sat in silence, not in fear but in faith, holding on to every last precious moment we had with him in this lifetime. We were mindfully aware of the spiritual transformation that was taking place, but we held on physically as long as we could, gently caressing his hands, telling him how much we loved him.

Suddenly Dad whispered, "They're here."
I asked, "Who's here Dad?"
With a look of pure amazement he said, "The angels."

His eyes were aglow as he studied heaven's door and then, without warning, the physical bond was broken. Dad released our hands, lifted his hands upward, and with his final breath, gently called out, "Ma... Pa."

His earthly journey ended as the angels, along with his mother and father came to lead him home, to meet the God he loved so much. With tear-filled eyes, Mom and I sat for what seemed like eternity, wrapped in emotional turmoil. With one brief whisper, Dad was gone and our lives were changed forever.

What a tremendous loss, yet what a gift. Faith, hope and love, the greatest trilogy of emotion. My dad who loved me unconditionally as only a father can love, who taught me right from wrong, and faith through actions, now gave me hope. Hope in eternity and in a world beyond our human experience. I found great comfort in knowing when it's my turn to meet Christ face-to-face my dad will be there with the angels to guide me home.

And love, what about love? Yes... as the greatest commandment proclaims, *the greatest of these is love.*

My dad's final gift to me was a clear understanding of faith, hope and love. The divine virtues I learned about in first grade catechism now have meaning and reveal the key to life and happiness. In Dad's dying, he was born to eternal life, and we observed the transformation of that process. This is an unmeasurable gift. I feel both honored and chosen to have witnessed one of life's greatest mysteries. Is there life after death? The answer lies in the gift. The answer lies in the whisper.

It is now up to us to share the gifts of faith, hope, and love with our world. As Mom and I experienced a glimpse of heaven that cold December night, we knew our lives would never be the same. Our experience was a genuine encounter with the Spirit of God and our calling is to share that light with our world.

Although my search for understanding and belonging had gone on long before, this story is the real beginning of my spiritual journey. Baptized a

Roman Catholic as an infant, I searched long and hard for the meaning of Christianity and for understanding of the spiritual realm. I searched from church to church, from denomination to denomination trying to find the secret.

In my head I understood that God loved me and I believed in salvation. I longed for a connection that would be nourishing and purpose-driven. But there were so many choices. Catholics, Fundamentalists, Protestants... Who was right? The more I searched, the more confused I became. There are so many variations of belief, each with rules and traditions of their own. Which ones are man-made and which ones are scriptural? Which translation of the Bible delivers the authentic word? My faith was strong, but I was weary.

When I stood at the podium and shared Dad's story with those who attended his funeral, I knew I had found my answer. The answer lies in our relationship with our God and the people we meet in our lifetime as we recognize the little piece of divinity alive in each of our hearts. This revelation brought clarity to my search. All along I had the answer; it lies in living out a life filled with faith, hope, and love – in being present for those placed on our spiritual pathway.

That December morning in 1995, I was filled with joy as we celebrated a life that had transformed my world. Do I miss my dad? More than anyone will ever know. But how can I be sad? Dad's whisper, *"They're here,"* has energized my soul and has assured me that I will see him again. We will be together forever in eternity, surrounded by the essence of the God we love so much.

The poem, *God Hath Sent His Angel* by Grace Noll Crowell[1], beautifully summarizes our experience. I concluded Dad's eulogy with the reading of this great work of poetry. As I moved from the lectern, the following words resonated in my heart for all time:

"An angel bent above him in the night
To strike his chains away and set him free."

---

[1] Crowell, Grace Noll. *God Hath Sent His Angel:* Compiled by Editors of Guideposts, 1993, p 38.

Dad is no longer restricted by the pain of disease or limited by the restraints of this world. His chains have been lifted. He is free to love for all eternity. Love transcends time and space. To witness the evolution from one lifetime to the next has brought me such comfort. Dad's presence surrounds me daily. The connection of love binds together both our worlds.

"An angel bent above him in the night, to strike his chains away and set him free." These words are engraved on my heart and will forever provide understanding of faith, hope, and love, with the greatest of these being Love.

Chapter Two - Gentle Man

In the midst of fear and uncertainty, he waited...days passed...
life grew fragile....a love so strong...a soul so eager to reunite,
yet limited by human understanding....hesitation to journey
forward... liberated by a single tear.

A few months after my Dad passed away I was in the midst of another typical day as Director of Operations for a senior home care agency. My morning schedule had me meeting with the daughter of a potential client who was currently in Hospice care.

The two of us sat at her kitchen table reviewing paperwork when she expressed a concern she had regarding her dad. It had been over a week since she brought him home from the hospital. The doctors expected he might only live a day or two. She wondered if her dad was afraid of dying. He was so frail she didn't understand why he was holding on to life. I listened, offering empathy and support, as she shared her concern.

Aware this was a short-term assignment, we agreed to start a caregiver the following day. Just a few hours a day would allow his daughter to run errands, get rest, and attend to the necessities of life.

She took me into the living room to meet her dad who rested comfortably in a hospital bed located in the center of the room. A credenza was placed at the foot of the bed with a picture of a woman positioned at eye level. Curtains covered the windows but the rest of the room appeared virtually sterile-like with bare walls and no other furniture. The woman in the picture was beautiful with a warm loving smile. A sense of honor and reverence appeared to surround her space.

As I watched this gentle man, somehow I knew that divine intervention had called me to this moment. I sensed that destiny had brought me here, and this meeting was part of my journey as well as his. I felt an emotional bond which led me to take hold of his hand, connecting us soul to soul. From this point forward I was aware of a spiritual presence and understood that God was in charge.

I asked him if the woman in the picture was his wife. With a smile he nodded, "Yes." I told him how beautiful she was and I commented on how much he must have loved her. He nodded as a single tear rolled down his cheek. I sensed a love beyond normal and a unity that few are blessed to share. As he looked at her picture, he said, "I am afraid heaven will be so crowded that I won't be able to find her."

With tears rolling down my face, I tenderly touched his hand. It was like touching the hand of Christ, that piece of divinity in each of our hearts, connecting us to the universal creator who gives us life. This moment took my breath away as I came to understand a love beyond intellectual comprehension.

I leaned toward him, my heart bursting with compassion and understanding and I asked if I could share a story with him. With his nod of approval, I shared my dad's experience and how his mom and dad came to take him home. Looking into his eyes I said, "You don't have to worry about finding your wife because she is waiting to meet you and to lead you home." He softly touched my hand as tears rolled down his face releasing all fear and limits of human understanding. He whispered, "Thank you."

We never placed a caregiver in his home. The reunion of this gentle man and his wife happened shortly after that transforming moment in time. Honestly I don't even remember what he looked like, or his name, but I can still take myself back to that moment in time, and sense the touch of his hand. My life changed forever that day as I came to understand the tremendous healing power in love.

When I left his home I could not pull myself away. I sat in my car, in his driveway, for an unconsciously long time. I had just met Christ face-to-face. The presence... the love... the awareness was surreal. I was not ready to come back to this earthly plane.

As I journey forward I recognize a need to trust, allowing the Spirit to take the lead when I am called to these divine encounters. When I do, I am overwhelmed by God's amazing love. It is such a tremendous blessing to share God's light with our world, making a difference, one soul at a time.

The seed of faith planted in me as a child is blooming. Hope is bigger than I can still comprehend. Our perception is limited by the human mind, but each spiritual encounter takes us deeper into our own understanding. Time spent with this humble man may have been brief but he touched my heart forever. The spirit of Love in his heartfelt words, "I'm afraid heaven will be so crowded..." moved me beyond measure.

What a gift I found in his whisper, "Thank You." No, *thank you* beautiful soul, for sharing with me the intimacy of Love. Yes for sure, the greatest of these is Love.

"An angel bent above him in the night, to strike his chains away and set him free." Is this a line from a poem, or poetry in motion? To release the pain, the fear, the uncertainty that stands at death's door, sets us free to love. Love never fails!

Chapter Three - Mary Helen

In the midst of loneliness... joy abounds...a welcoming spirit...a delightful soul... hallowed with remarkable memories...passionately embracing life and laughter...revealing purity of heart.

I was attracted to Mary Helen the instant I met her. She was one of those people whose spirit tugged at your heart strings. Mary Helen was eighty-nine years old when we met, filled with spunk and vitality. She loved life.

Scheduled for an introductory meeting, the message I received said she lived alone and needed someone to help with running errands and companionship. I knocked at her door and Mary Helen greeted me with the cheeriest, "Good Morning, please come in."

Dressed in her Sunday finest, as if about to go somewhere special, she directed me to her dining room table where she invited me to take a seat. The table, set with precision and care was both pleasant and welcoming. A vase of fresh flowers arranged at the center, sat atop an elegant lace tablecloth. The intimate setting highlighted a lovely china teapot and two matching cups and saucers which awaited our company. Small plates, with two cookies apiece, and linen napkins completed each place setting. It became inevitable this consultation with Mary Helen would be no ordinary orientation meeting, and we were about to have a very special afternoon.

Within minutes of sitting together, sipping tea, I felt the spiritual connection. I sensed this was a pre-destined meeting with the spirit of intention and purpose again knocking at my door. Some people are brought into our lives for a lifetime and others for just one season, long enough to inspire growth as we journey forward. Mary Helen came as my season of joy! A true pleasure to be around, she absolutely enjoyed life to the fullest.

Our time together kindled in me a desire to find contentment in the present moment. Mary Helen did not allow loneliness to control her state of mind. She easily could have, but instead, embraced life and made the best of her situation— aligning her heart with whom-ever God sent her way. We sat at her table for hours, just talking and laughing. In fact, we never got around to talking about caregiver services. That required a second visit.

Wow, what a storyteller! She drew me in on every word. She mesmerized me. Mary Helen loved sharing tales of her younger days and memories which shaped the confident, precious woman she had become. Her favorite story, which I invited her to tell each time we were together, made me laugh so hard I cried.

Mary Helen grew up in an era when life was much simpler. Her family lived in a small town where her father served as mayor. Back then townspeople were like family. Her dad, as mayor, became the father figure for the entire town. He had a genuine spirit of joy, and a charism much like the daughter he raised.

She told me the story of the time they built a new outhouse behind their home. Her father, so proud of the little house, invited the whole town to join them in celebration. Dressed up in their finest they assembled in the town square and paraded to the new outhouse location.

As the grand master of the parade, her dad led with plunger in hand, marching to the beat of the music. Oh yes, the local high school band took part in the festivities. In unison the family, band and townspeople marched through the streets until arriving at their destination, *the new outhouse*. Once there, they surrounded the wooden comfort station, saluting as her father pulled out the garden hose commencing with the initiation ceremony. Then she said, "Out came the food and drink and they partied all day, testing the function ability of the new structure. That is when the merriment began."

This story might sound silly or trivial, but I wish you could have observed Mary Helen as she told the story, with sound effects and motions. You would understand... had you seen her face, or heard her laughter as she shared her fondest memory. She was pure joy in action. There is a great message behind her story, one which encourages us to step back and celebrate the little things in life. Each time I asked her to share her story, she gladly obliged, charming me with her special gift of embellishing the details.

Our friendship blossomed over the next year as she influenced an attitude of joy in my life. I loved our time together, until one day when I received a phone call informing me that Mary Helen was in the hospital. Sorrow filled my heart as I held her hand and watched her struggle for life.

I tried to cheer her up by telling her the *outhouse story*. Her face lit up as she managed a brief smile, still sparkling–even through the pain. I'm not sure if the story itself amused her, or if my attempt at embellishing the details made her smile. I know for sure, in that moment, peace and unconditional love surrounded us, joining our hearts together forever.

As I reflect on our final moment together I recognize how blessed we were to have connected and found such a beautiful friendship. Through a saddened heart, with tear-filled eyes I whispered, "Goodbye my friend, until we meet again." In that moment, as we embraced, I felt purity of heart.

Psalm 126:2
We were filled with laughter,
and we sang for joy.
And the other nations said,
"What amazing things the LORD has done for them."

The Lord has done amazing things indeed! We are meant to share the joys of life so others may experience the love of God. Mary Helen did that for me by just being herself, her genuine, honest, sincere, wonderful self. Isn't that what we are all called to do? To be comfortable and confident with whom we are, and to be present in one another's lives– sharing our uniqueness and giftedness. Being open and evoking the person we were created to be is where we find– peace, love and joy!

Less than a year after meeting Mary Helen, I had the privilege of saying a few words at her funeral. What a beloved gift she was to me. Born in June, our last celebration together was her ninetieth birthday. Oh, how she loved life, being ninety, and having lunch together. Mary Helen was in my life for a brief time, just one season, but she will live in my heart forever. I am so grateful for her presence in my life.

We intimately connected; soul mates on a journey towards wholeness.

Aside from love, Mary Helen taught me many things. She taught me it is okay to use my fine china every day, and two cookies are all we need. I've realized that memories and love are all we can take with us as we journey forward into the kingdom. I've acquired a passion for the simple things in life and the ability to meet each person as if we were meeting Christ. Most important, she taught me to be joyous always. Mary Helen said, "There's always something to celebrate, and if there is not– create it."

Mary Helen died in August at the end of the summer season. Summer brings with it sunshine, blossoms, fruits, vegetables, picnics, parades, ball games, gatherings and much celebration. How appropriate God called her home in the season of such abundance of life. I am sure as she met the God of her understanding–she heard the words, "Well done my good and faithful servant, you have spread much joy to my people."

Journey on my dear friend until we meet again...

Chapter Four - Char

In the midst of painful memories...trapped like a time warp of the mind...wisdom reveals... the touch of the weaver's hand......gold and silver interweave... the soul takes flight.

The sun was shining, the air warm and breezy, my husband and I sat with our dear friends, Tim and Ginny, under the big old willow tree in their backyard. It was a beautiful summer afternoon. The day, like so many of our family gatherings included fun, love and laughter. Yes, family. With thirty years of friendship, Ginny and I consider ourselves sisters–sisters of the heart.

We enjoy many wonderful times together including vacations, spiritual retreats, parties, church and breakfast each Sunday. Prayer has sustained us through many of the challenges that parenthood and family generate, but we are absolutely best at celebrating. Plenty of practice throughout the years has made it a perfected trait. This particular day, we celebrated the end of an extremely hard winter in

Erie, Pennsylvania, and looked forward to the start of the long-awaited summer season.

I sat under the old willow enjoying the gentle breeze, engaged in conversation with Tim's mom, Char. I was unaware of the inspiration and encouragement which was about to come my way. Usually unannounced or unsuspected, a defining moment will suddenly present itself on our journey, guiding and directing us toward our purpose.

Char is a fun-spirited woman. Like Mary Helen in the last chapter, she can tell a story better than any other. When Char has center stage, she will not let you down as memories of the past turn into laughs of the day. Free-spirited at the young age of eighty-nine, competitive by nature, she still enjoys Scrabble, bocce, bridge and any other game, even some she makes up herself. She is wicked at knocking over bowling pins with a pair of pantyhose tied around her waist, and a potato tucked deeply into the foot. Anything for a laugh! She is a sweet, fun-loving Irish lady who is the center of attention at every family gathering. Give her a microphone, the rest is history. This is the Char I cherish and hold in high esteem.

The conversation under the willow tree presented her more serious side, one spiritual in nature. She is such a dear lady with a depth to her spirit and wisdom which time and experience has brought to fruition. We sat chatting about the happenings in our lives, catching up on family events. I mentioned my interest in writing and shared with her the progress of this book.

Catching me totally off guard, tears welled up in Char's eyes, as she whispered, "I once wrote a book." When she looked at me, her eyes revealed a deep-rooted pain imprisoned for a long time. She leaned over, touched my hand, looked me straight in the eyes and said, "Let no one stop you from writing, or deprive you of your dream." Goose-bumps ran up and down my arms as we connected. I placed my hand on hers curious to find out more about her book. When did she write it? What was it about? What happened to the book? In my heart I wondered what caused the hurt I saw in her eyes. An overwhelming spirit of compassion and empathy connected us on a much more intimate level as we embraced the strength and healing power of love.

Char explained that she was much younger when she authored her book. The theme of her manuscript was family. She shared with me how she had asked someone whom she loved and trusted to read her book. This person laughed at her, criticized her work and demeaned her effort. Offended and hurt, she put her book away, discontinued the writing process, and gave up on her dream.

Many years have passed, still deeply wounded–Char buried the pain, and stifled her creativity. My heart ached for her loss, yet I sensed her enthusiasm and her desire to help me on my journey. She encouraged me to move forward and to not let my dream die. Somehow I understood the wisdom which hid in her pain. I understand the mindless chatter in our heads that won't stop, regardless of our effort to tune it out and the self-doubt that circulates as we pursue our passions. It's our own ego which haunts us all.

How did she know my heart said write while my head said you are not good enough? I presume my eyes revealed self-doubt as much as Char's eyes exposed her pain. There is great revelation in the windows of our souls.

As we sat and talked for hours that summer afternoon, I saw deeply into the depths of her soul. I realized it was difficult for her to share such personal testimony, but being a master storyteller and a kindhearted friend I understood why Char was open to the opportunity. Her sharing, her touch, her tenderness was a tremendous gift. She inspired me and encouraged a determination to complete this project, for both of us. With faith and hope, I pray that through our sharing, Char has let go of the pain. I pray that God's transforming energy has inspired healing along with a new release of creativity.

We continued our conversation while Char gathered more information about my book. I shared my ideas with her and the stories of the first couple chapters. I also shared my title, *Listen to the Whisper.* As she listened, she said it reminded her of a prayer which she says each day entitled, *The Weaver.* I asked her to share her prayer with me and I promised to email her the first couple chapters of my book. She was excited to read them and offered to help with the editing process.

Following is her email response:

Hi Sandi! I've read the first chapters of your book, and you have been blessed to experience the work of the Spirit in your life. The stories are awe-inspiring and now you want to write about them, so that others may find inspiration reading your book. The content is very good, and there is no doubt you have talent for writing. I edited both chapters, being honest as you asked, because if you want to publish your book this is what will happen. It would be great if we could get together at your house as that is where you probably have used your own computer and would do the corrections and/or additions and deletions. Let me know when it is a good time to do this.[2]

Here is the Prayer I mentioned:

The Weaver
by Grant Colfax Tullar [3]

---

[2] Char, Erie, Pa, June 2014, Email received, Permission granted for publication.
[3] Tuller, Grant Colfax . "The Weaver". b. 1869.

"My life is but a weaving
between the Lord and me.
I cannot choose the colors
He's working steadily.

Oft' times He's weaving sorrow;
And I in foolish pride
Forget He sees the upper
And I the underside.

Not 'til the loom is silent
And the shuttles cease to fly
Will God unfold the canvas
And explain the reason why.

The dark threads are as needful
In the weaver's skillful hand
As the threads of gold and silver
In the pattern He has planned.

Her response inspired the pursuit of my dream. Her prayer, *The Weaving*, gave heart to my work.

The dark threads of Char's story are guided by the skillful weaver's hand. I am honored and grateful for their touch. When two souls unite in creativity and in love, they are like threads of gold and silver. Thank you, Char, for being gold in my life. You are such an important part of the pattern He has planned for me. I am blessed that your loom has not been silenced and your shuttle still flies high.

Char and I enjoyed our time together as we met for edit sessions. She is gifted with her editing skills and has challenged me on word choices; corrected grammar and offered an objective eye. Most important, she represents divine inspiration, as God unrolls the canvas and reveals how we can make beautiful colors together, fulfilling both of our dreams.

As my journey continues I learn to trust, to believe in myself and to respect the talents that God has given me. I have learned to hear the Spirit's whisper which is revealed through others who are placed on life's pathway. Listen for your whisper...

Chapter Five - Father Pete

In the midst of drug addiction, alcoholism and desolation...spiritual restoration and wisdom represent courage and possibility...a humble, soft spoken, passionate healer...shepherded by unconditional love.

With a temperature of one-hundred-four degrees, crippled by weakness, I found myself hospitalized with the doctors totally bewildered as to the cause. Time passed, my fever persisted and yet, no diagnosis. I endured test after test with multiple doctors, including an infectious disease specialist, and still no finding. Fear and trepidation consumed my every thought.

Finally after three days the doctors reached a consensus. Blood-work, multiple scans and tests showed definitive cancer cells, active and alive in my body. Surgeons were notified and on stand-by, one to perform the hysterectomy and another to remove the growth found on my intestines. Doctors were unified in their decision that we could not proceed until the fever was gone. So we waited. The fever remained despite the medication and treatment.

The next evening as my mom, aunt, and husband John spent time with me, a special visitor arrived. Surprised to see Father Pete, I questioned how he knew I was in the hospital? Aware of the great work he did, serving those with drug and alcohol addictions, I knew of his busy schedule. Why would he take time to visit me? I later found out a friend of mine, Joe, who served on the board of trustees for Father Pete, had asked him to come.

Father Pete laid his hands on my head and said, "I understand you are in need of a healing." He asked my family to hold hands, and join him as he prayed for healing of body, mind and spirit.

Leaning over my bed, he whispered in my ear, "Cancer takes a miracle, do you believe?"
I nodded, "yes."

He smiled, while he continued to pray. When finished, he asked my mom and aunt to leave the room. He talked with my husband and me privately, persuading us to have faith in the power of God's grace and miracles. Father Pete believed and trusted I would receive a complete healing.

He questioned me, "When you receive this miracle, do you promise to dedicate your life to God?" Of course I said, "Yes." Without further conversation, he left my room.

Bright and early the next morning, the nurses appeared to deliver the good news. My fever had broken through the night. With my temperature back in the normal range, the surgeons were called and arrangements made for back-to-back surgical procedures to happen that very morning. My fever was gone the morning after Father Pete's visit–was this coincidence or divine intervention? I did not have much time to think about it as they wheeled me off to begin preparing me for surgery.

John, my mom, and children were with me that morning. Frightened by the unknown, we hugged, cried, prayed and expressed our love for each other. It's difficult to wrap your emotions around cancer without generating anxiety and fear. My son, the last person I saw before the anesthesia kicked in, was so scared. With worry in his eyes and tears streaming down his face he choked out, "I love you, mom!"

It appeared just minutes had passed when I heard them calling my name. Recovery already? Upon opening my eyes, the nurse said, "All went well. I'll get your husband for you." Together we tried to process everything that had transpired as we waited for the surgeon. What exactly did she mean–*all went well*? The time passed slowly. We waited.

Now back in my hospital room, we were told the doctors were on their way. First we spoke with the obstetrician & gynecologist who had great news. The ovaries were full of cysts, it was necessary to do a full hysterectomy, but no cancer existed. She reiterated the concern she had going into surgery and expressed how pleased she was with the outcome. Before leaving she smiled and acknowledged that we should give thanks for the gift we received.

Soon afterwards, the general surgeon arrived. As she sat on the edge of my bed, she took hold of my hand, looked directly into my eyes and said, "You must be a believer." Upon examining the intestines, there was redness as if something had been there, but further examination revealed nothing. *No tumor! No cancer!* With tear-filled eyes she articulated, "A miracle–this is the only explanation I have, there is no other answer." The scans identified the tumor– the blood work confirmed the counts."

Both surgeons were so compassionate and convincing in their belief of the gift I received. Was Father Pete the catalyst of a miracle? Did healing energy channel through this gentle, humble man, granting me the gift of life?

After trying to process and absorb the reality of this miraculous occurrence, John called Father Pete to share the good news with him. He listened as John talked, then merely said, *"You sound surprised."* He instructed John to remind me of my promise.

Home for six weeks recovering, I spent a great deal of time trying to understand all that took place. Was it just a figment of my imagination or was this tangible evidence of a God greater than anything we could ever imagine? My childhood beliefs of religion and a God somewhere in the heavens, were transforming into a spiritual understanding of a God alive and present with us today.

When Father Pete prayed with me at the hospital, he asked if I believed. So if this belief (faith) was strong enough to heal cancer, what more could faith accomplish? Father Pete so freely shared unconditional love and his healing energy with everyone he met. He went out on house calls to initiate healing and to spread hope to a hurting world. In return he asked that we trust God and give back. So what was I expected to give? If I shared this story would anyone really believe me? How could a prayer and a gentle touch heal cancer?

On my final day at home before returning to work, there was a knock at my door. Standing unassumingly on the other side was Father Pete. I'm not sure which surprised me more, his presence at the hospital or his presence at my home. He had a way of sneaking up on you when you least expected it. As he entered my living room he announced that he came to collect on my promise, and he reminded me of my agreement to give my life to God.

Then he released the bombshell, the lightning bolt if you will. He said, "I came to invite you to join us in prison ministry." Prison ministry? "Oh, no way! No, Father, not me, anything but that." With a sheepish smile on his face he said, *"No' is not an acceptable answer.* You can't turn your back on a promise." So there began my interest in prison ministry and working with drug addicts, alcoholics and those most in need of faith, hope and love.

I'm not sure which was scarier, hearing the word cancer, or my initial encounter with a prison, but my heart has been renewed and a great change has taken place. In prison we call it *Metanoia,* a Greek word meaning *change of heart.* If we listen, we are all called to a Metanoia. We are called to progress on our journey. When working in the prisons we tell the inmates that the greatest distance anyone has to travel is from their head to their heart. When our faith finally comes alive in our heart, great things will happen. Unconditional love lives there and is ready to shepherd us and heal us– body, mind and spirit.

Father Pete is the most influential person I have ever met. As time went on, he became my spiritual advisor and mentor. He was a man of few words, but the words he shared were profound, thought-provoking and life-giving. He encouraged a life filled with the Spirit, a life of simplicity and grace. Material things meant nothing to this humble man. Touching souls was the only reward he needed.

After almost fifteen years of working together, our leader and friend was ready to enter the Kingdom, as God called him to new life. We wanted to do something special for him, acknowledging his presence and importance in our lives. Visitations, understandably, were limited to immediate family members.

So, after much deliberation a group of us agreed to a grand serenade. Father teased us often about staying on pitch when we sang, but he loved to sing praises which made this the perfect gift. We stood outside his bedroom window on a cold, rainy May morning and sang his favorite hymns. I'm not sure there was pitch or harmony at all, as we choked out the words to his favorite hymn...

Praise God from whom all blessings flow...

Tears flowed like the rain upon our backs. Father looked out the window, smiled and waved his sign of approval. This simple offering exemplified Father's lifestyle, one of simplicity and love.

Monsignor James W. Peterson, as the obituary read, was lovingly referred to as Father Pete. He may be gone from us physically, but his spirit lives on in the many courageous souls he touched, as they continue to believe and explore the possibilities.

Chapter Six - Tommie

In the midst of fear and anxiety...negative imageries...meta-morphosized by a calling...abundant treasure...new life...a mountain top experience with views of the kingdom.

Believe me when I say that *fear* is not a strong enough word to describe my feelings as I entered the prison for the first time. My mind was my own worst enemy, creating illusions of evil, imprisoning me in my own reflections of despair. Images of criminals, rapists, murderers and thieves controlled my thoughts and inhibited my ability to reason. I walked the long sterile hall, with my heart in my throat and then I heard the slam, the lock of the metal door behind me, and reality sat in quickly. There was no turning back, so I prayed, "Come Holy Spirit, fill the hearts of your faithful..."

A local county prison provided the setting for my first encounter with prison ministry. Soon after meeting the inmates, my preconceived ideas and fears vanished as I came to understand that inmates are just people, no different than you or me. The mistakes they made may have been larger, or perhaps they just got caught. Nonetheless, their needs, and ours, essentially are the same. They want someone to believe in them, to talk with them, and listen to their stories, without judgment.

Our first Metanoia, in that county prison, introduced me to a robust, strong, tough looking African American man named Tommie. He may have had a rugged and threatening outward appearance but I knew within minutes of meeting him, that his inner-self resembled that of a giant teddy bear. His jovial personality and spirited demeanor captivated me instantly.

I came to find out that Tommie and his many brothers and sisters grew up in the south raised by a single mother. Together they lived in a one room, mud-floored shack. There were no beds; they slept huddled to keep warm, on a cold dirt floor. He attended school through the third grade. Their mom would wake them up in the middle of the night to go out to search for food and whatever else they could find necessary for survival. Poverty defined their destiny.

Tommie sat next to me during the four-day Metanoia weekend. He was fun to be around, cheerful by nature. He had an eminent ability to make you laugh. During the weekend the team presented the inmates with letters, written by members of local churches, meant to offer support and prayers. They were a source of encouragement for them and a lifeline to combat seclusion. When Tommie received his letters, he leaned over and whispered, "Miz Sandi, I can't read. Would you read them to me?"

This happening caused a transformation to take place in my heart and prison ministry almost immediately became a new passion. Men and women called to different ministries often talk about *The Calling*, which I never understood. Initially when I agreed to serve on the team, I did it out of obligation, returning a favor for the healing I received. That soon changed as I came to understand *The Calling*. My heart felt it! The Spirit of God called me to this new ministry, to serve men and women who are otherwise shunned by society.

From that point forward determined to do all I could, I wanted to help make a difference in their lives. I no longer identify inmates by their crime; I recognize them as men and women of God. They, like us, were created by a loving God and struggle to make sense of life. I am honored to serve those most in need of mercy.

As the weekend continued, besides reading Tommie his letters, I helped him learn the songs. I would put my arm around him as we shared a book, pointing at each word as we sang, hoping he would learn to recognize the words. A relational bond formed, comparable to that of a mother and son. I watched as Tommie experienced a Metanoia. He had a true change of heart. He experienced God's love in a profound way... as did I. The smile on his face brought such joy to my heart, like watching my own son walk across the stage at graduation.

On Sunday morning Tommie came to the table with a drawing he made for me. It was a colored pencil drawing of a rose, on yellow lined tablet paper. He said, "Miz Sandi, I drew this for you." The gift was better than silver, crystal or gold. I related it to the woman in the bible who freely gave her last two coins. Tommie did the same as he gave all he had to give. That picture hung on my refrigerator door for years representing the simplicity God calls each of us to live– a life of love.

Often when I am called to grow or move along on my spiritual path, I find myself arguing with God. "No not me– not that Lord!" Once I give in and accept the challenge, the Spirit leads me on some exciting adventures. The mountain is often used as a metaphor for life, teaching us that we don't grow on the mountain top; rather it's the climb upward that builds our strength. I have realized I need to stop arguing with God. When I am called, I've learned to accept and to say, "Yes," and brace myself for the climb. My journey has been amazing and spectacular just like the view from the top of the mountain.

Tommie's pencil drawing is one of my valued treasures. It represents the release of fear and the beginning of new life. I know his climb is much more difficult than mine. I understand why the Bible tells us in Matthew 20:16, "The last will be first, and the first will be last." Being born into poverty was not his choice. Survival demands action. What chance did he ever have?

Conceivably, Tommie will live out his life as part of the penal system. I can only hope that something from the Metanoia weekend has brought him into relationship with a loving God who can lead him to new life. We may not meet again in this lifetime, but I know our souls will rejoice when we are reunited in the kingdom. This thought fills me with tremendous joy and energizes me into the future as I anticipate great things yet to come.

Tommie's Drawing

Chapter Seven - Ed

In the midst of razor wired fences, steel bars and correction officers...peace and tranquility find rest...in a modest wooden chapel...talents...purpose...passion...come to life...bestowing a wealth of grace.

Prison ministry has evolved for me, moving from county prison to state and federal institutions. Fear tagged along for a brief time with each new endeavor. Our humanity drives our emotions, so I've learned to stop beating myself up, and to just acknowledge the feeling. For a while, I thought of fear as a weakness but with time I've learned that fear can actually strengthen us. As we learn to release the fear and to support love instead, we find respite and strength in the release.

In the late nineties, we received an invitation to attend an annual retreat at a maximum security prison in central Pennsylvania. Father Pete asked us to sing at a Forgiveness Ceremony on Friday evening, and to attend the Saturday morning closing festivities of the week-long retreat. As you read previously in an earlier chapter, *no* was not an acceptable answer when it came to Father Pete.

Among our group of friends involved with prison ministry, the men from the group had been participating in this particular retreat for a few years. Now, the institution agreed to permit women volunteers into the facility for the first time. I must be honest, the words *maximum security* automatically produced thoughts of anxiety and fear.

To add to our emotions we found the chapel located near the back of the property, making it necessary to walk a long distance through the open prison yard. With inmates unaccustomed to women volunteers, you can imagine the stares and remarks we received as men literally lined the pathway. The negative energy could have sent us running in the other direction if love did not prevail.

Once inside, a warm welcome from the chaplain and the employed inmates helped to restore our sense of intent and purpose. The chapel, simple, yet beautiful, evoked a sense of peace and serenity. It has the capacity to house approximately three-hundred people while still preserving an essence of intimacy one might expect from a small sanctuary. We learned the history of the *All Faith Chapel*, constructed entirely by the inmates in the year nineteen-sixty-four. A spirit of ownership still motivates the inmates' desire to worship, and it encourages them to invite others to be part of the sacredness of the space which their peers skillfully crafted many years ago.

Friday evening as songs of praise and worship filled the air, we came to appreciate the spirit of God's love so present in that little chapel. We looked out at the men in their brown uniforms with DOC (Department of Corrections) written across their backs, they humbled us by their presence and their respect. The retreat team encouraged each man to approach the altar and kneel before a cross. I don't believe there was one man who did not come forth. They journeyed onto their knees voluntarily, one at a time, seeking forgiveness from a merciful God. With humility and honor, they accepted the grace and love of God as they moved toward complete surrender.

We renamed their uniforms. To us, DOC now stands for Disciples of Christ. Their dedication has moved us to new understanding of surrender. For survival within the prison system they have had to learn, all-too-well, the necessity of submission. They have built-up walls and hid their feelings to prevent further emotional pain. Yet here in this chapel, in front of guards and other inmates, we witnessed complete surrender and their yearning for forgiveness. They wept openly allowing their walls to crumble, exposing vulnerability in their ominous surroundings. I felt blessed to witness such exemplary faith, hope and love in action.

I received another special gift that day when I had the privilege of meeting Ed. As we sang, I glanced out and saw him sitting half-way back, leaning against the end of the hand-crafted pew. We made eye contact and smiled at each other. Once again, I had the same sensation I always experience when I know I am called to connect with someone on a spiritual level. When the ceremony ended, I went over to meet him. Fortunately we had a few minutes to talk before the guards summoned the inmates to return to their cells.

The next morning at the closing ceremony, I was pleased to sit next to Ed. We had time to talk as we waited for the service to begin. He shared portions of his story with me and told me he was serving a life sentence. I found it difficult to comprehend that he could have done anything serious enough to warrant a life-sentence; he appeared to be such an easygoing person with a kind, gentle nature. We worshiped together. The time flew by so quickly. Before we knew it, the service had finished and the guards promptly directed us out the door. I told Ed I looked forward to seeing him the following year. His response was, "Three-hundred-sixty-five days until we meet again. I'll be counting the days."

Later that year, Father Pete informed us that the prison administration had nominated Ed for commutation. His reputation was remarkable as he maintained a perfect record, even after serving almost thirty years. To this day, Ed remains in high-regard, clear of any violations. He is a hard-working, model inmate who believes in the power of prayer. His leadership skills help him find purpose, as he guides others to the chapel, encouraging them to find the peace that passes understanding.

His commutation paperwork, completed and signed by the higher officials of the prison, sat on the governor's desk for a long period of time awaiting his official stamp of approval. After many lingering months, Ed received notification of the denial of his commutation. His life sentence would stand.

Long after the Governor received Ed's paperwork, the Board of Pardons accepted a new amendment, modifying the Pennsylvania Constitution. The reformation called for a "unanimous recommendation," for the commutation of a sentence of death or life imprisonment– a majority vote would no longer suffice. [4] If that wasn't disheartening enough, the new regulations also stated that inmates who were serving life sentences could no longer work outside the physical walls of the institution.

Ed loved his job working in the apple orchard. As you may have already suspected, the orchard is outside the prison gates. "Where is the fairness in this," I ask? Not only was Ed denied commutation, in

---

[4] Pennsylvania Board of Pardons, 1997, Information Retrieved at http://www.bop.state.pa.us/portal/server.pt/community/history/19511

addition, he lost the job which connected him to nature, sustaining his peace and tranquility. Wasn't thirty years enough of a sentence for a man with such an impeccable record? What more proof of reformation and rehabilitation did they need?

When we returned to the prison the following year, shortly after Ed received this debilitating news, I expected to find him discouraged and depressed. Instead, I found him sitting in his same seat, wearing the same gentle smile. How was it possible for him to be so peaceful? Had being institutionalized all these years, stripped him of his emotion?

As I spoke with him, I asked, "Ed, how can you be so happy?" He faithfully said, "It's clear God needs me here more than he needs me on the outside." Wow! His faith is beyond human comprehension. Ed is a man of great character and I am blessed to call him friend. God continues to enlighten me, sending people of light and love my way. This clearly was a defining moment for me. Ed represents the ultimate lesson in humility, and taught me it is possible to live in-the-moment, and to be happy regardless of circumstances. I have discovered that relationships are the treasures of life and if we are open, we will meet unconditional love face-to-face, in the most unlikely places.

On one of our return visits, Ed presented me with a gift. He painted, with oils, a picture of a stunning Indian girl. He told me, before coming to prison, he couldn't draw a stick figure. It is amazing, how with God's touch, our talents are discovered one brush stroke at a time. Ed spends much of his day painting which provides stillness and quietude in a hostile environment; it also supports his divine purpose. God bestowed on Ed a passion for serving others and the ability to create beauty via his artwork. When I look into the eyes of the Indian girl in the painting, I connect with Ed's soul. They bring to light his hidden pain, yet at the same time the wealth of grace which has supremely set him free.

Someone once asked me, "What is the opposite of love?" I thought the answer was hate, but I was wrong. I came to understand the opposite of love is fear. For me, prison ministry has proven this lesson true. I walked in through the barbed wire with a heart filled with fear. Touched by the Spirit of a grace-filled

God, I left with my heart overflowing with unconditional love and a renewed appreciation for the little things I often take for granted.

I think of Ed often, praying that someday he could be released. I would love for him to live out his final days in freedom. Then I ponder, "What is freedom anyway?"

Freedom is a tranquil state of mind. The choice is ours for the taking.

Painted by Ed in December of 2014
"Listen to the Whisper"

Chapter Eight - Bethany

In the midst of confusion and uncertainty...solitude and spiritual direction tug at our hearts ... a soaring eagle... set us free... stillness and serenity take refuge... ordinary miracles brought to light...oh the places we'll go...

My job as Director at the senior home care agency was enjoyable, I loved it, yet I felt a yearning to move forward. A sense of restlessness emerged– I had this inner-feeling which would not go away. It appeared I had come to a crossroad on my journey– confused and unsure of what to do I sought the help of a friend.

My soul-sister and dear friend Judy, a counselor and teacher by trade, listened as I voiced my concerns. She encouraged me to spend time in discernment before making any decisions. In fact, she suggested getting away for a couple of days, and offered to join me at a retreat center in Frenchville, Pennsylvania. A week later with arrangements made, bags backed, and Judy's guitar in-hand, off we went on an uncharted adventure.

We planned a self-directed format, allowing time for whatever venture the spirit sent our way. Bethany (the retreat center in Frenchville) is located on a beautiful piece of rural property and is run and operated by four sisters of the Anawim Community. It offers trails through the woods to a mountain top cross, outdoor Stations of the Cross, a labyrinth, a grotto and a chapel. The location provided us ample space for quiet reflection and the perfect place to learn to discern.

The following scripture verse greets you when you enter the Bethany website:

Come, let us climb the Lord's mountain...
to the house of the God of Jacob,
that he may instruct us in His ways,
and we may walk in His pathways. Isaiah 2: 3[5]

The first thing we did, as soon as we arrived, was climb the Lord's mountain. It was a picturesque autumn day, with crispness in the air. The trees had already shed their leaves, creating an ambiance of

---

[5] Homepage image. Bethany Retreat Center, Retrieved from http://www.bethanyretreatcenter.org

solitude. We walked, talking very little, savoring the stillness of the hill. Once at the top, we discovered a wooden bench with a clear view of the mountain top cross and a panoramic view of the valley. We sat reflecting on nature's beauty when an eagle flew above the cross, soaring gracefully through the sky. Oh, to fly! The freedom... the majesty... the grace...

A favorite scripture verse came to mind:

Isaiah 40: 31
Those who hope in the LORD
will renew their strength.
They will soar on wings like eagles;
they will run and not grow weary,
they will walk and not be faint.

Seated at the top of the hill I understood Isaiah's declaration regarding walking in his pathways and being instructed in his ways. In the stillness we gained peace; in the flight of the eagle, promise to be free.

After a contemplative afternoon, we stopped by the office so I could schedule an appointment to meet with Sister Therese for spiritual direction. Fortunately she was there when we arrived, giving us the opportunity to meet before our session. The connection was immediate as I shared with her my quest for discernment and the inner-restlessness I sensed inside.

The next morning as I arrived for our meeting, Sister mentioned she had come up with an idea after thinking about our conversation from the previous day. She started by telling me in all her years of doing spiritual direction, she had never once asked anyone to leave Bethany's grounds, but, that was exactly what she was asking me to do. She invited me to trust the Spirit's lead and to journey with her to another location.

The next hour we talked about discernment and direction, and various ways we could identify whether our thoughts were our own ideas or God's plan. Sister addressed my apprehension and the message the Universe delivered through the eagle at the top of the hill. It was one of the most enlightening hours of my life. Mindful of a new sense of discovery and direction, we agreed to join Sister Therese on her proposed adventure.

Immediately following our meeting, we were off on our spirit-filled quest to an unknown destination. Judy and I met Sister at her car where she informed us of the day's events. She explained we would be dropped-off for a few hours, but not to worry as *they* were expecting us. She would take us back to our retreat at Bethany as soon as we were finished. We had so many questions. Finished with what? They, who were they? She wasn't staying? This definitely took trust but at the same it stimulated excitement. Is this what it felt like to be free– to fly like an eagle? Unbeknownst to us, we were about to soar to new heights.

We pulled up to an old run-down, but well-kept home in the middle of town. A woman, close to our own age, greeted us at the door. Sister Therese did her introductions and off she went, leaving us to find purpose in God's plan for us.

There is an agape love, a spiritual and selfless kind of love, that can only be experienced in a woman's shelter. Sister took us to a place where women and their children recovered from abuse and despair. This safe haven directed them towards hope and guided them as they worked toward rebuilding new and restored lives. We sat and talked with the women who bravely shared their stories. They displayed such courage as they openly communicated their dreams of a brighter future. We helped in the kitchen as the women prepared dinner for their children who were soon to return from school.

Oh, what joy filled the room when the children came bouncing in, so happy to return to a place of protected refuge. It was here we met the young teenage girl who endured immense tragedy in her young life, yet inspired us with her resiliency and positive attitude. The abuse left behind disfiguration and horrible scarring of her face, arms, and backside. She described how her father poured boiling hot water on her in the midst of one of his many fits of rage. I cannot imagine the agony this poor girl had to endure. Although anger and resentment seemed justified, she embodied bravery, confidence, and self-assurance. The other children looked up to her as she displayed genuine leadership qualities. This young lady represented heroism in our eyes.

She shared with us her love for singing and her wish to audition for a singing competition. Her wish, turned into an afternoon of great fun. We encouraged her to sing for us, which took little prompting. Before long all the moms and their children were gathered around the kitchen table singing *Amazing Grace.* As Sister Therese walked in the back door she found the house filled with laughter and sounds of praise. She had a huge smile on her face as she greeted everyone. She looked at us and said, "I knew you belonged here."

We rode back to Bethany in silence as our day concluded with an essence of *Amazing Grace.* I reflected on Sister's reaction and her comment. What did she mean, "We belonged there?" My thoughts kept returning to the young girl with the scars and burns. At such a young age, in spite of her violent past, she appeared to be so confident. Her story disturbed me, yet I acknowledged a tugging at my heart to do more. We bonded with this young girl.

The weavings connected as the whisper of God's voice explained the restlessness that summoned me to Bethany. Spiritual presence again called me to new beginnings, the tapestry soon to be unfolded.

Just days after returning home, I received a phone call from a friend. He served on the Board of Directors for a local women's shelter, and he called to tell me they were looking for a Director of Operations. He knew nothing of my experience at Bethany– he merely believed this position might interest me.

The little piece of divinity in each of us, which connects us to something greater, goes beyond belief. Some may call it coincidence but I'll leave that open for your own interpretation. Judy and I referred to them as *God Winks*. This experience took my faith to the next level and gave me a deeper understanding of the power of surrender and trust. I never understood discernment. My strong will always led me to decisions long before I listened for God's answer. My experience at Bethany taught me to slow down and sit in stillness, present to the beauty of creation around us. In the stillness we hear God's whisper.

My time as Director of Operations at the local women's shelter was a life-changing experience. Judy came to work as a volunteer, and together with my husband, the three of us led a spirituality class once a week. The song, *We Will Rise Again,*[6] along with the scripture reading from Isaiah 40, served as a theme leading the women to be free, and to run and not grow weary. They learned to find strength in a God that loves them unconditionally, and to move forward to rebuild the fibers of their lives. With God, all things are possible!

Although we started out believing our retreat at Bethany was self-directed, it didn't take long to discover who truthfully guided our journey. The women of the Frenchville women's shelter profoundly changed my life. They helped me to re-direct and identify the Spirit's call to action.

At Bethany, I also acquired an interest in writing. The evening after meeting with Sister Therese, words kept dancing in my head as I tried to sleep. I couldn't turn them off, so I got up and put pen to paper. In a short time the following poem was created:

---

[6] Composed by David Haas, "We Will Rise Again", 2012.

Ordinary Miracles
Sandi Matts

Ordinary Miracles at Bethany,
Tugging at our hearts to set us free.
A hundred forty acres on a rim,
Four brazen Sisters of Anawim.

A slow leisure walk going nowhere,
Magnificent evergreens dance mid-air.
One lone bird, flying yet still,
High above the cross at the top of the hill.

Laughing with serenity; stories re-shared;
Unloading burdens, no longer scared.
Hand carved treasure; Eucharistic Gold;
Iconic paintings; Miracles behold.

Ice crystals in the Labyrinth of time;
Silent spoken words, gifts divine.
Two graceful deer running free,
Across a frosted field of our memory.

Snow turned to sunlight with the blink of an eye;
Holy Spirit soaring like an eagle on high.
Sedentary visit; chapel at night;
Speak Lord, we're listening, our futures in sight.

Smile from a soul-mate; a silent meal;

Contemporary stations help us heal.
Mantra reflection; candle aglow;
Prayer shawl solace; blessings bestow.

Spiritual direction; contemplative prayer;
Young families singing; soothing despair.
A shelter, a prison, a pregnancy in need,
Direct us Spirit, we'll follow your lead.

Ordinary Miracles at Bethany,
Tugging at our hearts, Amen, we're free!
A hundred forty acres on a rim,
and Sister Therese of Anawim!

Our journey is amazing and the intricate plan that God has put together for us progresses beyond human understanding. The coincidental encounters with people and destinations are elements of the labyrinth of life. As we turn each corner we are not sure if we'll run into a road block or a clear passageway. We just need to continue. As I reflect on this thought, I think of the popular children's book entitled *"Oh the Places You'll Go."* [7] With simple illustrations, Dr. Seuss so profoundly teaches us to move forward and to experience all life has to offer. Oh the places yet to go...

---

[7] Dr. Sues. *Oh, the Places You'll Go!*, Random House 1990.

Chapter Nine - Juanita

In the midst of co-dependency and imprisonment...isolated and alone...fear and anger nestle in comfortably...desire and forgiveness triumph...love permeates, and the music plays on.

Oh the places you'll go indeed! So with excitement and enthusiasm I began my new job as Director of Operations for a local women's shelter. A small intimate room, located on the second floor behind the bathroom and across the hall from the library/chapel/music room, became my new office. Throughout my year of employment with the shelter I had many wonderful conversations in that tiny office, great one-on-one time, where I got to know the hearts of the women who took refuge there.

One such woman named Juanita came into the program directly upon her release from the county prison, where she served time for drug related activities. She came, broken with fire and anger in her eyes, not prepared for what she was about to encounter.

My position awarded me the opportunity to work with the residents on financial matters, beginning with the process of developing a budget. I remember Juanita's initial response when she learned the rule which stated that she needed to account for every cent she spent. Let's just say cooperation was not a learned skill for Juanita, and a hardened heart did not allow her to follow direction.

After a short-time at the house, Juanita agreed to attend the spirituality classes that Judy, John, and I offered weekly. We shared our eagle story, from Bethany, which seemed to stimulate a desire for rebirth. With time, Juanita transformed her way of thinking, and allowed a break-down of some of her walls. She loved singing songs of hope with the group, and the positive environment of the sessions. God whispered her name, and she listened. Her climb was not easy, but she persevered.

Juanita is bright, creative and talented. It was essential for her to believe in herself and to learn to accept her giftedness. Juanita grew up with a passion for music. Involvement in her high school band and the ability to compose her own musical arrangement's, was instrumental in her receiving a full music scholarship at a college in Arizona.

When Juanita left her family behind and chose the road of drugs, she also left behind her music and the opportunities it offered. Juanita's choices led to years of alienation from her family, her music, and the beautiful person she is. Eventually addiction became her identity, and her choices led to her incarceration.

I was on duty the day Juanita received the news that the courts were terminating her parental rights and her three youngest children would remain in foster care and would be put up for permanent adoption. I believe this was her ultimate moment of despair and the loss which touched the core of her being. When she opened the letter which delivered the dreadful news, she fell into my arms and sobbed. For the first time, Juanita let her guard down allowing herself to feel the pain, also to accept the love I offered.

This was a real turning point! A moment of truth! Soon afterwards, Juanita made the decision to stop fighting the program, and to work with the counselors in getting the help she needed. She learned to process her thoughts and she slowly allowed positive feelings and emotions back into her life. She journeyed through her heartache and losses and embarked on a path of self-forgiveness. As she let go, one step at a time, she accepted herself as someone of worth and value.

Over time, Juanita's newly found self-worth resulted in positive changes. Music came back into her life as she played the keyboard again. A decision to go back to school awarded her with a CNA (Certified Nursing Assistant) License. Hired by a local rehabilitation center, Juanita gained self-confidence as she helped others. The very judge, who sentenced her to jail, provided a life-defining moment, as he hired her to care for his own father, in his own home. What a tremendous gift that judge gave her! What a tremendous gift Juanita gave that judge! An extraordinary amount of healing occurred as they trusted each other.

Juanita has had to overcome many obstacles on her journey, more than most. A reconnection with her family, (her mom, brother, sister, and two daughters from a previous relationship) continue to play an important role in keeping her accountable to her sobriety. Love has become her new lifeline, inspiring her to stay connected.

Relationships are an important part of all of our journeys, and forgiveness is an integral part of being able to love. Juanita now understands that her family never stopped loving her. It may have appeared that way to her, but it was essential for them to give her space and time to make her own decisions. They gave her wings (like the eagle) so she could find her own way. Juanita and her family now enjoy a deeper appreciation of love. Mercy, love and forgiveness set them free to be family again.

Now celebrating eight years of sobriety, Juanita bravely shares her story of heroin addiction and the climb to new life. In doing so she continues to build strength, comprehending the full value in relationships and helping others. Life has come full-circle for Juanita as she now works as a residential manager at a woman's shelter. In addition, she is attending college pursuing a degree in criminal justice aspiring to work as a drug and alcohol counselor. The struggle to find balance is a daily event, but I know she will succeed because gratitude lines her course and she lives a God-centered, purpose driven life.

Centered on top of her piano, she bravely placed a picture of the three children whom the courts took away from her. As she plays, she prays! If it's God's plan, she knows they will someday reunite giving her the opportunity to tell them how much she never stopped loving them.

Integration back into a society which once shunned her, offers hope to those that hear her story. No one can be taught in a classroom what she has learned through life experience. Her spirit of courage to overcome will transform the hearts of many as she pays forward the many blessings she has received along the way.

As mentioned previously, some people come into our lives for a season, and others are there for a lifetime. I am so privileged to have Juanita as part of my family, for a lifetime. With a grateful heart I give thanks for her presence in my life and for all she has taught me.

In the year Twenty-Twelve, Juanita received *The Spirit of Courage Award*.[8] This award is presented annually, through the Sisters of St. Joseph, to a recipient who has showed outstanding courage. It was one of my greatest pleasures, and such an honor, to nominate and present her with her award. Juanita is truly my inspiration!

My time of working at the women's shelter came to an end after just one year. Administrative differences led me to walk away from my position with a very heavy heart and a sense of failure. As I walked out the door, it was Juanita who stood in the hall with tears in her eyes, encouraging me to keep my chin up.

Through prayer as I struggled to heal, I realized the Spirit led me to the shelter so I could meet Juanita. I also recognized that God led Juanita there so she could meet me. Now, years later we both are grateful

---

[8] Sisters of St. Joseph, Spirit of Courage Award, Retrieved at
http://www.ssjerie.org/support-us/spirit-of-courage.php

for fate as we celebrate its call to purpose. I am so in awe as I comprehend the great instrument of Love, and its life-changing power. Relationships are like melody and harmony, both instrumental in playing out the music of our souls.

One hug, in a moment of emotional despair, connected Juanita and me for a lifetime. The hug she returned as I walked out the door, assured me she felt the same. She got it! I got it! Crescendo!

Oh the places we will go... as the music plays on...

Myself, Juanita and Judy
"Spirit of Courage Award Ceremony"

Chapter Ten - John

In the midst of blisters and pain...Native American Spirit beckons... Spiritual awakening sustains attraction...love triumphs... gratitude re-energizes...happiness prevails.

Blisters produce pain! Healing of the blisters restores appreciation for healthy feet. Gratitude for the healing presents a flow of positive energy. Attention to the positive energy signals a release of more positive energy. In very simple terms, this describes *The Law of Attraction.*

Recently my husband, John, and I traveled to Denver, Colorado for the Hay House Writer's Conference. Neither of us had been to Colorado before so we went out a few days early to tour the area. On our second day of the trip, we traveled from Denver to Estes Park and Rocky Mountain National Park. There is no way to capture or express the beauty we experienced.

Painted across the crystal blue sky, the white snow-capped mountains provided a breath-taking view. The sound of the raging Colorado River was life-giving, its force capturing its power. Over many years, melting snow carved spontaneous waterfalls into the rocky knolls, which summoned a call to peace. The wild life roamed free and unafraid. Colorado is a place where humankind and nature interweave– creating a universal energy of tranquility and love.

We walked for hours that day. In fact my Fit-bit (step tracker) logged in over twenty-thousand steps. This is how John's blisters developed. We spent the morning in Estes Park leisurely walking along the River Walk, strolling through the unique shops. John, wearing a brand new pair of sandals, had two huge blisters sculpted into the sides of his feet. By lunchtime the pain summoned his attention. Luckily I had packed Band-Aids, antiseptic cream and sneakers. We doctored up his wounds and journeyed forward with our day.

For over five hours we traveled the nineteen mile path through Rocky Mountain National Park, stopping and walking at each lookout point along the route. John was a real trooper, trying hard to focus on the positive energy that surrounded us instead of the pain he felt in his feet. We would later understand the purpose for the blisters and pain, but first we needed to accept, focus, and listen to the "voice of" Mother Nature.

The strangest thing happened as we trekked through Colorado. Everywhere we went it appeared a raven was following us, more specifically John. The first day in Colorado Springs, he mentioned a raven flying overhead. We watched it fly so freely across the red rock formations. The second day in Estes Park, a raven followed our trail along the River's edge, following us into Rocky Mountain National Park. As we stood at one of the lookout sites, a raven circled above us, this time cackling *"cras... cras."* It definitely insisted on our attention as it swooped within six inches of John's head and hovered there for a moment. Wow! Okay, Universe– you positively have our attention.

That night, while in the car heading back to our hotel in Denver, I surfed the Internet, reading aloud everything I could find relating to the ravens.[9] We

---

[9] Raven Symbolism and Symbolic meaning of Ravens by Avia Venefica, Retrieved from http://www.whats-your-sign.com/raven-symbolism.html

learned they are humanitarians symbolic of mind, thought, and wisdom. The ravens are bringers of light which summon a spiritual awakening. Native American Indian lore describes ravens as creatures of metamorphosis symbolizing change and transform-ation. They are called upon in Native ritual for healing as they help expose the truth, essential for health and harmony. They are credited for bearing magic, and harboring messages from the heavens, whispering to those worthy of the knowledge. What knowledge was John worthy of receiving? What message was the raven whispering to John, to us?

On our flight to Colorado, John shared how he looked forward to spending time in nature and connecting to the Native American spirit so prevalent in the Midwest. He couldn't wait to spend time in the mountains, to commune with Mother Earth and to slow down the pace of our busy lives. But I, as an activator, planned daily explorations touring the entire area. God had other plans, and I can't believe I'm admitting this, but John was right, we needed to slow our hectic pace.

John's blisters were symbolic of the pain and burdens of life which we tend to hold on to forever. Our most recent problems included the heartache of a son recently hurt by divorce; the stress of John's job now switched to second shift– lessening the time we spend together; and upcoming decisions concerning retirement. The pain of the blisters forced us into slowing down, long enough to listen, enabling us to hear the raven's healing call of the Universe. Mysticism surrounded us exposing the truth. Our metamorphosis occurred with the renewing of our minds and acceptance of what life had to teach us. The process unearthed balance, and healing of our bodies, minds, and spirit.

The next two days I attended the writer's conference and John spent time alone. He read, slept, and hung out at the pool, soaking up the healing energy that comes from stillness. I believe we both received the same message from the raven, a call to "Be Still."

Our experience in Colorado reminded us to live by the Law of Attraction bringing the essence of appreciation back to the forefront. We have much to be grateful for including a marriage of forty years. It wasn't always easy but love made it worthwhile. Back in the difficult years, when we focused more on the negative, conflict and disharmony emerged as a way of life. Since practicing the Law of Attraction our marriage has evolved into a sacred union. We are now connected with God, each other, and the Spirit of the Universe creating a whole new understanding of the language of love.

We have two wonderful children and three grandchildren whose exuberance for life has brought true joy into our lives. Family is holy and life-sustaining, nurturing the love which dwells in the heart of each of us. We have the most amazing friends! They are a tremendous gift to us, bound together by a spiritual depth which only time and love can develop.

Messages from the raven clearly reminded us we didn't need to look further than our own front door. We already have everything we need. God, family, and friends are the Band-Aids and antiseptic which help us rise above adversity and pain. We are so grateful. Love is the answer! Love is the secret to attaining peace and happiness. It sounds so simplistic, but is it? If it were, would we need the metaphor of the raven? Why would there be anger or hatred in our world?

For now, our hearts are rekindled with universal love. Sitting atop our metaphorical mountain, we are energized by its majesty and power. Gratitude carries us forward exposing the possibilities yet to come.

As John loaded the suitcases into the car at the end of our trip, he heard the familiar *"cras… cras."* He looked up and sitting on the hotel's roof directly above him, sat the raven. It cackled loudly, I believe John did too, as they looked respectfully into each other's souls. Recognizing the connection, they communicated their good-byes and set each other free to journey onward wherever the Spirit led.

Ravens really are magical. We really are magical. The Universe and Creation are there to set us free!

Chapter Eleven - Fred and Father John

In the midst of an uphill trod...coached by an athlete, scholar and saint...the athlete in me takes notice...I am moving...I am winning... perception shifts...with fortitude I cross the finish line.

"How bad do you want this? Stretch it out! Come on you can do this!" These are the words my race coach Fred used as encouragement while we ran the second annual 5k event at our church.

As far back as I can remember, every July our church hosts an annual chicken dinner/festival. We serve the most delicious chicken in town, cooked by our local firemen on open charcoal pits. Hundreds of people come from all over to enjoy the festivities, the good food and friendly atmosphere.

Last summer our friend, Peggy, shared her vision of families coming together the day before the festival, to engage in outdoor fun and exercise. When Peggy introduces an idea, she sticks with it until her plan is fulfilled. Hence, the inaugural *Winner, Winner, Chicken-Dinner Run/Walk* launched that very summer.

Last year John and I entered and walked our first ever, 5k. Mostly fellow church members took part, with everyone high-fiving, cheering and celebrating along the route, making it invigorating and joy-filled. John and I were content with our time, coming in under an hour. The event was a huge success, so the committee agreed to make it an annual event.

For me, this event stimulated an interest in taking part in other 5ks in our region. Last summer I ran/walked in five different races. The atmosphere at these events is always great fun. There is a powerful vibe which runs through the air and a dynamic that is unmatched.

As I walked, I reflected on Father John's inspirational words. He is the spiritual director who took over prison ministry for Father Pete. Father John gives many talks during a Metanoia weekend, but the one which motivates me most is the one which challenges us to be athlete, scholar and saint.

When he begins his talk, he travels around the room and asks the inmates to call out names of athletes. The shouts begin: Michael Jordan, Tiger

Woods, Ben Roethlisberger, and so on... He goes around again and probes for names of saints, and they respond: Saint Paul, Saint John, Saint Mark... When he requests famous scholars, they answer: Aristotle, Socrates, Einstein...

He does a second sequence, this time directing them to choose someone from the room who is an athlete, a scholar and a saint. The challenge becomes much more difficult at this point; envision men, incarcerated, demeaned daily by their peers, the penal system and their world. Father asks them to make a list of their three top weaknesses and in a matter of seconds, lists are complete. However, when he invites them to list their greatest strengths and attributes, they cannot comprehend and most are not able to list even one. Father John challenges them to value themselves and to recognize the giftedness they each represent. Imagine the transformation when they shift their thinking and open themselves to discover their own goodness.

Father gives the example of his own morning routine. Each day at five a.m. his alarm summons him to run three miles, establishing the athlete in him. He shares with the men, "I don't compete or try to break any records. My sole purpose is to care for the body God gave me." He tells us, "We are all called to be athletes."

After his run, he returns home to spend time in prayer. Meditation is his time to talk with God, and to listen. He instructs the men on the importance of taking time to be silent. He reminds us, "We are called to be saints, to care for our soul."

Next, Father John reads every morning. He articulates, "Don't read garbage and don't read the negativity that's in the daily news. Read something of substance that is thought-provoking and stimulating to your mind. We are all called to be scholars and to take care of the mind God gave us."

We are preordained to be athlete, scholar and saint. It is essential to our well-being we care for our body, mind and soul. I ponder this daily as I strive for balance in my life. Each part of the formula is of equal importance. Father John has found the answer and is dedicated and faithful to his routine. It is a daily challenge, but I am trying and I value and grasp the worth of this life-giving formula. Last summer when I started taking part in 5k events, I contemplated Father's words. Maybe I am an athlete... a scholar... a saint. A desire for balance stirred in both my heart and soul.

I have now participated in a dozen or more 5ks with the best time of fifty-one minutes. Not great, but not terrible for a sixty-plus year old woman just getting started. The most important thing is I am moving, working on balance and having fun at the same time!

The thought of having fun brings me right back to Fred and the *Winner, Winner Chicken-Dinner 5k Run/Walk*. The first quarter mile of the race I sprinted, enjoying the exhilaration of the run. Within a quarter mile I slowed to a quick walk to catch my breath. This is where I ran into Fred, a fun-loving guy with a warm-hearted, welcoming spirit. As you may have detected, I am drawn to people who love to have a good time. Fred fits that bill, so we walked and talked.

He spoke of Kay, his wife, who at the young age of sixty-nine still wins most races she enters. They ran together as a couple for over thirty-five years, in fact, they met while running. Unfortunately, Fred's back and knees can't take the pounding any longer, so he walks... he walks extremely fast.

As I tried to keep pace with Fred, I realized we were walking much faster than my normal. I shared with him that my best time was fifty-one minutes. He asked me if I would like to better that time. He shared that his usual time clocked in around forty-four minutes. Wow! That's fast. So, I aligned my stride with Fred, and the race was on!

We hit the one mile marker when they called out, "14:26!" I did the math in my head (the scholar in me) and I recognized I could finish in forty-five minutes or less if I continued at the same pace. So I set a goal and welcomed Fred as my coach. He cheered me on every step of the way. If I fell behind, he urged me to run. When we arrived at a flat grade on the route, he shouted, "Are you ready? Let's run!"

If I lagged behind, he cried out, "Do you want this?" He'd encourage, "Stretch it out, you can do it!" He instructed me to stop pumping my arms so high, I was wasting energy. For the first time in my life, a spirit of athleticism arose in my soul. Oh, I golf and played basketball for a while in high school, but I never experienced such personal concern from a coach. Fred's mission was to help me be the best I could be, not to come in first or win medals. He has a zest for life and the ability to make a person feel important and loved. Honestly, my spiritual journey took a leap forward that morning, as Fred exemplified the lesson of athlete, scholar and saint.

Divine intervention helped me correlate this experience to the guys in prison. I know how much I enjoy helping and coaching them to be all they can be, but I never understood, from their perspective, the emotion of being on the receiving end. As Fred coached me, in his unassuming way, he helped me to realize a level of humbleness and gratitude for the people that God sends our way. Fred escorted me to a higher state of understanding and taught me if I want something, and I want it bad enough, it's there for the taking. To have doubts in ourselves is part of human nature, but God calls us to believe in ourselves. When we do, it's quite an adrenaline rush. Father John, I get it. The feeling is amazing! I am an athlete.

As we run, walk or partake in any sport or exercise, we awaken the athlete. We qualify right now for the race. I get it, finally. All we need to do is put one foot in front of the other and move along, doing the best we can. If we believe in ourselves, we will find success. When we rid ourselves of negative self-talk and focus instead on positive beliefs, it's there we will recognize the spirit of God that lives within our own mind and heart.

In addition, I am a saint. Whether I help the guys in prison, or I am alone in meditation, I am a saint. The afternoon following the race, my friends and I had the honor of singing for the funeral of a dear friend's mother. As we sang, I connected the thoughts. In giving of ourselves, we pray– thus in giving, we are saints.

A scholar is defined as a specialist in a particular branch of study. Therefore, as I travel on my spiritual journey, opening myself to the possibilities, as I turn each corner of the maze of life, and I study and listen as I go, I establish myself as an expert or scholar, and God fills my heart and soul with good news and wisdom.

Sometimes God speaks to us in a whisper, riding in on a lightning bolt, lightly delivering the message. If we do not pay attention, He may have to raise his voice, demanding our attention with the startling boom of thunder. I get it, God, I heard the thunder and I believe. I am a winner, an athlete, scholar, and saint... right now, just as I am.

When we approached the second mile marker, the time keeper yelled out, "14:02 keep going." I shouted, "Yeah Fred, we got this, we're faster than the first mile!" My enthusiasm to finish under forty-five minutes increased, adrenaline pumped, and my competitive spirit stood at attention. Fred said, "Do you want this? Then let's run." So we ran, then we walked, and forward we trod. There was the finish line, within reach. I could see it, it was so close. So, I sprinted as Fred exclaimed, "43:04!" 43:04! I did it! No, we did it! Coach Fred and I celebrated. Two minutes under the goal we set, and seven and a half minutes better than my all-time low, what an amazing day.

A high-five and a victory hug followed. We had much to celebrate. Fred didn't know it at the time, but he knows it now, we are both *Athlete, Scholar, and Saint* and we get it. Thank you, Fred, for being part of my race... It was a blast.

Thank you, Father John, for the great life lesson on how to sustain balance of mind, body and spirit. This is our divinity, our connection to God the Father (mind), God the Son (body) and God the Holy Spirit (spirit).

Chapter Twelve - Sophia

In the midst of a circle...vision and dreams become reality...friendships flourish... attitudes of optimal well-being...channel healing energy... unwavering faith and divinity...weave onward towards new life.

When I think about balance of body, mind and spirit, my immediate thoughts are of *Sophia's Circle,* my small Christian community. Nineteen beautiful women make up this spirited prayer group which has been together for twenty-five years. Visions and dreams become reality among *Sophia Sisters,* and I cannot imagine life without them.

Sophia has inspired me to live life by the famous words of Ralph Waldo Emerson who said, "Do not go where the path may lead; go instead where there is no path and leave a trail."[10] These women have adopted this attitude and are trailblazers among our larger community and peers. A state of optimal well-being is a little easier when interconnected with such a nurturing and supportive network of friends.

---

[10] In January 1992 an academic periodical called the "Middle School Journal" printed the saying with an attribution to Ralph Waldo Emerson. Reference at: http://quoteinvestigator.com/2014/06/19/new-path

The energy of the group is diverse, with each woman contributing her own unique gifts and talents. Collectively we embrace a sense of wholeness and vitality which inspires our desire to help others in finding balance of body, mind and spirit. We remain freethinking and unconventional, but holistic in our aspiration to tap into *the Source* of divinity which connects us all.

One member of our group, Sharon, is a licensed counselor and spiritual healer. She brings to the group a greater consciousness and recognition of our spiritual gifts. Her guidance helps us to accept our own potential by channeling God's healing energy through various media.

An introduction to the practice of *hands-on-healing* inspired the inner healer in each of us. Sharon brings her healing table to the two overnight retreats *Sophia's Circle* attends each year. With her leadership, we practice and explore the ancient tradition of energy healing. At first, the concept was foreign and uncomfortable, but within a short time we recognized and accepted the energy source. The light of Christ revealed the sheer energy and power of our touch. As we released the fear of the unknown, comfort and understanding opened our hearts to the calming and therapeutic value of human-touch.

Little did we know our new skills of healing were about to be tested. I clearly recall the disturbing phone call I received from Liz, one of Sophia Sisters. She sounded weak and broken. She wept as she told me she had been to the doctor's office that afternoon and received a diagnosis of stage IV non-Hodgkin's lymphoma. I listened, we cried together, and I struggled for words. What does one say at a time like this? I reminded her of the love and support of our group and encouraged her to join us at prayer group which was held at my house the next day. When I mentioned that Sharon would bring her healing table, Liz promised to attend.

With unwavering faith and a spirit of belief, in something we were still trying to comprehend, we prayed together. We laid hands on Liz and like never before, we prayed with intensity and fervor. That night, *hands-on-healing* went from something we learned, to something that changed lives. It certainly changed *Sophia's Circle* forever.

We wrapped Liz in a shawl lovingly made by the *Prayer Shawl Ministry* of our church. It continues to be a visible sign of the love we all share. Its warmth provided comfort whenever Liz felt alone. She shared how the shawl helped her get through the dreadful chemotherapy treatments while comforting her with an awareness of God's healing presence. She understood the faith, hope and love it represented as she focused on the healing not the cancer.

When Liz walked in the front door of my home that night, exhaustion and feelings of fear, anger, and hopelessness consumed her. When she got up from the healing table, undoubtedly a miraculous healing had taken place. An emotional and spiritual transformation had occurred right before our eyes. Liz's tears gone; the look of horror and fear wiped from her face, replaced with a tender look of inner-peace. It was an amazing moment, a sacred moment!

Each of us, personal witnesses to the power of God's love and grace, matured in faith that night. As

God's energy flowed through our hands we experienced oneness which connected us intimately with each other and with the <u>Source</u> of divine energy.

Sharon, whose vision and dreams were to start a healing ministry at our church, watched us grow in knowledge and understanding throughout the process. Manifestation of her dreams became reality after speaking with our Pastor. He gave his blessings on the start-up of a healing ministry and encouraged Sharon to offer workshops to train the healers. Many members of Sophia's Circle attended the sessions and now are part of the viable healing ministry at Our Lady of Mercy (OLM) Church in Harborcreek, Pennsylvania. "Go where there is no path and leave a trail!"

The night of healing at my home brought about a recollection of the healing I had received so many years ago. I phoned Father Pete and asked if we could organize a healing mass to support Liz. Father was in agreement and we selected Avila as the location. It is the retreat house Sophia goes to every April. We invited Liz's family, *Sophia's Circle* and our spouses, and Liz's closest friends.

Words alone cannot express the splendor, the love, and the magnificence present in the room that evening. We sang and prayed together, invigorated by the healing energy. As Father Pete laid hands on Liz, with our hands extended towards her, there was a unity which almost demanded healing. There were many tears shed that night, but not from Liz. She still sustained a sense of tranquility and peace, which empowered her inner healer to unite with its <u>Source</u>.

That night she heard God's whisper. Her storm appeared out of nowhere; but in the midst of being open to friendship, love and support, the healing voice of Christ whispered her name. As Sophia walked with Liz on the teetering edge of her storm, God revealed our own whispers of healing, second chances, and new life.

Liz and I both recognize our blessings. We are grateful for the most amazing support system, our Sophia Sisters, and for the unconditional love of a God that has gifted us with wholeness and complete healing of body, mind and spirit. Yes, Liz's lymphoma is in complete remission and has remained there for over eight years.

The Sophia Sisters have now entered into an incredible phase of our lives. Retirement has happened for many, but still looms in the not-too-distant future for others. Grandchildren have become our new topic of discussion, bringing joy beyond measure to our lives. Story after story of the great things little ones say and do, offer us hours of laughter. Sophia knows how to laugh as we have learned to not take life too seriously. In doing so our hearts are full… and our journeys move forward!

Trailblazing continues as we search to *Discover the Woman Within*, a series we started for the women at church. Each year over a hundred women come together to meditate, heal, and hear stories of faith, hope and love. We have connected not only with the women present, but with the spirit of women who have paved the way and gone before us. We pray the chain of love will continue as we leave behind our legacy of strength and love, connecting us to generations yet to come.

Sophia's Circle is blessed indeed as the journey of *Discover the Woman Within* continues. We know we are called to grow again. When God heals, we are asked to give back by serving others. This past season we have reached out across international boundaries helping women around the world. Members of the group have become part of making dresses for the girls in Haiti, where tens of thousands of people had lost their possessions when their homes collapsed in the earthquake. Others have supported a group of Ugandan women by selling their jewelry, so they can educate their children and themselves, taking women from poverty to self-sufficient life styles.

We have learned the importance of weaving, as presented in Char's prayer (Chapter Four), creating patterns of silver and gold, with the canvas of life open for discovery. We have discovered that opportunities are endless as we take hold of the Spirit's lead.

Margaret, Joanne, Carole, Sharon, Ginny, Linda, Mary-Ellen, Patty P, Patty M, Patty S, Deb, Liz, Ellen, Rose, Barb, Jean, Beth and Shelly: I am honored to call each of you friend and I love you from the depths of my soul.

Chapter Thirteen - MeMe

In the midst of emotion and tears…unparalleled joy swaddles the heart…generations shift course…grandparents are born…newborn touch…unmeasured love…memories erupt into a pot of gold.

Say, "Grammy!" "MeMe." Say, "Grammy!" "MeMe." This is the story of how I became MeMe, to the three most special little people in my life, my grandchildren, Brody, Abigail and Addison.

It was May in the year two thousand and seven, somewhere in the middle of the night, right around two a.m., when the phone rang. Mom, "I'm at the hospital." At the hospital! Oh… Oh, I'm on my way. I called John who worked third shift, and he said, "I can leave as soon as I finish this job." Finish this job? What? Our grandson is being born! Get home. I called my mom, and at the good old age of seventy-eight, she was at our home, dressed, hair done, and lipstick on before John even made it home. I guess it's a woman thing.

Eventually we were on the road, heading south on Interstate 79 toward Pittsburgh, Pennsylvania. We had only been traveling about thirty minutes when my cell phone rang. I looked and there was a picture of our daughter Kelly, holding the most beautiful baby boy I have ever seen. Tears of joy erupted instantaneously, I was a Grandma! We were Grandparents! The excitement of that moment is pure elation. Without a doubt, there has never been a moment in time more special in our entire life. Well, that is until I got to hold him for the first time, or feed him the first time, or read him his first book, and on and on... Life will never be the same. Yes, first-time grandparents really are ridiculously pathetic.

The next hour and a half seemed like eternity, but eventually we arrived at the hospital with my heart thumping and about to explode, we took the elevator to the maternity ward. We turned the corner and there they were: Kelly, Patrick and my new grandson. Grandson! Oh how I love the sound of that! It was difficult to see through the water in my eyes, but I heard my daughter say, "Meet your new grandson, Brody." Brody... what an adorable name. I soaked up the intoxicating fresh baby scent and the hypnotic sound of the infant coos. He was so precious.

Without thinking, I put my arms out and said, "Can I hold him?" I saw the look of love in her eyes as she drew him in closer and said, "Mom, I can't give him up yet." More tears of joy... what beautiful, heartfelt words from the birth of a mother. Unconditional love had taken hold of my daughter's heart, that moment took my breath away. I bent down and hugged and kissed them both, fully appreciating the special bond of love.

An hour later, Kelly moved from delivery to a regular room and we got our opportunity to hold Brody. We cuddled him, touched his soft, tender face, and examined his ten little fingers and ten little toes. We tried on our new identities, Grandma and Grandpa. They fit perfectly!

Holding a grandchild for the first-time generated a whole new meaning to healing touch. Nothing can compare with the gentle touch of a baby to connect you with the quintessence of a loving God, the energy is miraculous.

When I reflect on that day I am still amazed. It takes me back in time to Kelly and Patrick's wedding where I fondly remember them dancing their first dance as husband and wife. They twirled around the room, looking at each other with passion and tenderness in their eyes. In a room filled with hundreds of people, they were totally alone. They affectionately sang to each other the words of *Amazed.* [11] One of those tender moments in time, I'll never forget. Now, another memory forever encapsulated into the treasures of my mind. Brody's birth, an inaugural event, as it marked the dawning of a new generation. Kelly, you are the best daughter, wife and mother. Baby, "I am amazed by you."

In that moment I realized I was at a crossroad of a new phase of my life, and somehow I understood things would never be the same. I was so ready to jump into uncharted waters with both feet forward.

Brody is already seven years old. Where has the time gone? It is such a joy to watch him explore life

---

[11] Written by Marv Green, Aimee Mayo and Chris Lindsey, Recorded by Lonestar, "Amazed", released in March 1999.

and to watch his body, mind and spirit develop. He is in first grade and so smart– when he sets his mind to something, nothing stops him. From the time Brody was born, until this very day, he will not attempt a new task until he knows in his mind first, that he can do it. He is a strong-willed child, creative, passionate and loving by nature. His competitive spirit will be his strongest asset once he learns to channel the energy. I thoroughly enjoy being a spectator on his journey.

The gift of life is miraculous and inspirational, as each generation carries us closer to pure unconditional love. I've always loved my mom, my dad and grandparents, my brother, aunts, uncles and cousins. There was a safety and a security always present as they surrounded me throughout my lifetime. Then I experienced a new side of love when I met John. This love was different; there was a desire, a romance, a yearning for intimacy. Yet the same sense of safety and security embraced its existence.

Love came full circle for us as we welcomed our own children into the world. When I looked into the eyes of Jeff for the first time this indescribable emotion, a deeper sense of love, just occurred. I believe God awakens this instinct in us at the moment of birth, to fortify the safety and security of our own individual family. It's a natural, innate affection that connects us to the sacredness at the heart of this new fragile creation. What a tremendous blessing.

This love helps us change dirty diapers at two in the morning, and wipe runny, snotty noses clean. Love is the <u>Source</u> we entrust our children to when they grow and embark on their own journeys. It helps us to not become overwhelmed by the immense Godly task of raising children. Parent love changes everything! We learn to derive our sense of safety and security from trusting a power greater than ourselves.

God has a great sense of humor. We are given these children to care for, but we get no practice. God says, "Here they are, enjoy, do your best." Parenthood is the most important job of our life, yet there are no classes or lessons to prepare us. No instruction on what to do for teething, or potty training, or fevers over a hundred. We are on our own to handle temper tantrums and wounded egos when they don't make the basketball team or... But somehow, we develop with time, and we survive and even flourish.

In looking back, I realize we learn and practice on our firstborn. For sure, I did. So, I would like to take this opportunity to apologize to my son, Jeff, for the mistakes I made. Thank you for your patience with me. I did the best I could. I am so proud of the wonderful man and father you have become.

As I observe you care for Abigail, I find fulfillment in my role as a parent. You do a tremendous job in caring for your daughter which helps me believe that we did something right. I understand it can be overwhelming in your role as a single dad, but as I watch you so unselfishly give up some of your favorite things to spend time with Abigail, I know she will be just fine. You get it Jeff, you embrace unconditional love, and you accept its challenge.

It makes me so happy to see the twinkle Abigail puts in her daddy's eyes and I am so grateful for the wonderful gift they both are in our lives. Abigail is such a sweet little girl, so playful by nature. I love seeing her climb trees, and pick up rocks looking for worms, just like Jeff did when he was a toddler. Divorce can be difficult for the children involved, but as I watch her toss rocks in our pond, I envision her tossing away any pain and hurt she may have endured. As time passes, I believe Abigail will find her voice. She is developing into a strong and confident little girl, the exact things which make great leaders. She is open and loving. I pray that God will guide and direct her to become all He created her to be, and will lead loving people into both their lives.

Addison, our little bundle of joy and energy, completes our immediate family. She is a precocious child, spunky, passionate, adorable, and full of life. When they travel to Erie for weekend visits, I love greeting her at the door. She leaps into our arms and squeals, "MeMe." "PaPa." She makes us feel as if we are the most important people in the world. Her smile sets our hearts on fire.

I love being a grandma! I am perfectly content spending the rest of my life being ridiculously pathetic and moving forward to each event that lies ahead. We will take center stage cheering on each accomplishment and milestone in Brody's, Abigail's and Addison's lives.

As I reflect and give thanks for these three precious gifts, I listen for God's whisper. I wait... no whisper. There is no thunder or lightning. In fact, there is no storm. Grandchildren are the rainbows that come after the storms of life. They light up our life and fill our lives with multi-color. They are God's promise of new life and they help us live it abundantly.

When we follow the rainbow we are led to the pot of gold on the other side, and we find it filled to the rim with treasure. It's filled with Love... Pure Love... God's Love... the purest gold of all!

Chapter Fourteen - Mom

In the midst of family and love...purpose energizes reality...blessings conquer fear...memories stimulate richness... heart rates soar...in the twinkle of an eye...we dance on.

"I am so blessed!" As I began writing this book, my Mom became my biggest supporter and my faithful fan. She eagerly waited for each chapter to be written and then she insisted I run a paper copy over to her house as soon as I finished. By the time I got back home, my phone would ring and Mom would be on the other end singing my praises.

Everyone needs a cheerleader to encourage and motivate them across the finish line. Mom, the finest, most enthusiastic cheerleader, never spoke a negative word, even before the edits. She reassured, supported and with each chapter came the same assessment, "Perfect! Beautiful! I wouldn't change a thing. I am so proud of you." Then she would ask, "Who is the next chapter about?"

From the start, I intended for my final chapter to be Moms story. I planned a big *reveal* celebration– I would take her to lunch, present her with the story and watch the surprise as she read her name. Eager to write it and excited to see her reaction, I had already planned and outlined the chapter. It was the only section yet to write, when life took an unexpected turn.

The day of the funeral my daughter said, "Mom, Grandma knows, she helped you, she wrote the last chapter." Nothing can prepare you for the loss of a mom. It was so unexpected.

We thought she had the flu and had become dehydrated. We were sure she would bounce back, as she always had before. Not the case, this time. Two weeks ago today, the day I wrote Mom's Chapter– my Mother went home to be with the God she loved so much.

I began this book with the story of my Dad's passing and how the angels, and his Mom and Dad, welcomed him home. Although my heart is heavy and a tremendous sense of emptiness surrounds me, I am comforted by the idea of Mom and Dad together again. I have a sense of their spirits, connected by love, dancing through the heavens forever into eternity. My vision of their new dwelling place is perfection, brilliance, and freedom from the limits of this world. What lies ahead on their journey? What purpose will their souls encounter?

Mom left behind a fundamental but essential legacy. She taught us to love! Everyone that knew her was familiar with her renowned saying, "I am so blessed!" Mom lived by that motto. She looked for the blessing in all things, good and bad. I've learned through her example that, *blessed* really is a matter of perspective.

My brother Jim and I stayed by Mom's side in the emergency room, she was in tremendous pain. Devastated by her diagnosis of renal failure we recognized the severity of her condition. Mom did not have the flu. Her kidneys were in failure and the immediate need was to conduct an ultrasound to determine the cause, and a treatment plan.

Since Mom broke her hip a few years ago it became difficult for her to lie on her side. Now in order to scan the kidney, that was exactly what they needed her to do. So, Jim and I helped by rolling her and holding her up from the backside. We supported her as they took the pictures. Mom never liked to complain, but she moaned, "Oh! I feel so awful. Oh, that hurts." When they laid her back down she looked up at Jim and me, with such love in her eyes, she said, "I am so blessed." Even in the midst of pain and struggle, she recognized the love we shared in that moment. Blessings and love truly are a matter of perspective. It's in the eyes from which we see. Mom, Jim and I are the ones who are blessed– for having been loved by you.

Like the message we received from Father John in Chapter Eleven, my Mom's perception equaled that of a scholar. She lived a simple life but in a profound way. The philosophy she modeled her life after, could possibly change the world. If everyone focused their energy on love and family, and reflectively made them priority, war and hatred might cease to exist.

The Friday night before we took Mom to the hospital, I brought her to my home so she wouldn't be alone. Weak and exhausted, she spent most of the evening asleep. When she was awake, she reminisced about her childhood. What a blessing I received that night as I listened to her remarkable stories.

One story began with this statement, "I know when I was growing up we didn't have much, but I always thought we were really rich." I asked, "How's that Mom?" She then shared her story, telling me it was one of her fondest memories.

She mentioned special treats which Busia and DziaDzia (Polish for grandma and grandpa) made for mom and her siblings when they were kids. They made them with scooter pie irons. She told me the irons were round not square, but somehow her mom fit the square bread into the round irons. She then stuffed them with a small spoonful of pie filling. They cooked these little pies right on top of the stove, in their kitchen. Mom said, "What a treat. When we had those pies, Wow! They were so special. I knew for sure we were rich."

It's all perspective. I strive to have a positive outlook recognizing the great richness I have in my life. Love... it's all about love... simple love. Simple love (as in scooter pie irons) provides unmeasurable blessings. Blessings are everywhere, every day– we just need eyes to see.

My Mom led me to believe I was the most important woman on this entire planet. Our families were her purpose for being, and love defined her motivating source. Gratitude for such a magnificent role-model drives my passion to do my best in all things. Our family will hopefully uphold Mom's legacy of love, touching one soul at a time.

On July twenty-sixth, Mom's final day with us, she gave us actual physical proof of the power of love. When we arrived in the emergency room, I received a text message from my daughter, Kelly. She sent a picture of her and her children, Brody and Addison, with big cheesy smiles. The caption said, "We love you, Busia, get better!" When I showed Mom the picture and told her what it said, her response was surreal. She looked at the picture, smiled through the pain and said, "They are so precious!" As she spoke, her heart rate (in a split second) went from eighty-five to one-hundred-eighty-five. She kissed the phone, handed it back, and her heart rate went right back to eighty-five. Love… Love changes everything!

My Mom's heart… loved… love. She loved giving and did so until the very end. Her final words whispered softly and deliberately were, "I Love You." She then gently squeezed our hands, closed her eyes and took her final breath.

1 Corinthians 15:52
It will happen in a moment, in the blink of an eye, when the last trumpet is blown. For when the trumpet sounds, those who have died will be raised to live forever. And we who are living will also be transformed.

In the blink of an eye, Mom was raised to new life. She was called home and welcomed into the loving arms of the God she loved so very much.

She was also reunited with the love of her life, my Dad. I envision them in paradise, waltzing the night away on the universal dance floor of life. Serenaded by the most delightful, celestial choir of angels, I imagine Mom dressed in a flowing white gown and Dad's charming smile lighting their way into eternal bliss. They dance on, admired by those they so freely loved and served. Dance on Mom and Dad... until we meet again.

I intended for the chapter to end here, but Mom had one more message. She visited me in my dreams, the night after I wrote this chapter. She awakened me from a sound sleep in the middle of the night. I heard her voice clearly say, "Hey, Sandi." She sounded just as she did when she called me on the phone. Her voice, clear and strong, sounded healthy, happy and much younger. I asked, "Mom, is that you?" She simply said, "Nice job... Beautiful!" I asked, "Nice job with what Mom?" There was no further communication, but I knew the answer.

Goose bumps ran up and down my entire body. I felt her presence! What a glorious surprise and *reveal* it turned out to be. Her reaction was more wonderful than anything I could have ever imagined. Mom knew the last chapter was her story, and she still remains my biggest supporter and faithful fan. Perfect! Beautiful! Love from heaven... *I am so blessed!* I will love you forever Mom... My heart overflows...

Three Generations – Hanging on to Love

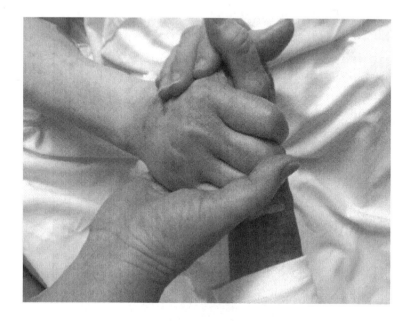

Final Chapter

Life is relational! People come and people go. Life plays on interweaving its lessons. With each lesson we grow and learn and accept all that we are. With each relationship, we connect and learn to give and receive, both vital in finding our purpose.

In this age of technology I like to think of these experiences as a means of creating our individual and unique spiritual data base, a collection and accumulation of information which we draw from and add to constantly throughout our lifetime. This data base stores and provides the pertinent information necessary for success on our journey. It collects names, experiences, relationships and words of wisdom.

This data base, which is updated daily, supports the development of our individual qualities such as faith, hope and love. All three are words of action which can be achieved through relationships, as proven by the people mentioned throughout the chapters of this book. As I look back and reflect on each person, I am confident they have each served a divine purpose in my life. God, who loves me, has placed them on my pathway to help fulfill my destiny.

I am so grateful and honored to share the stories of some of these wonderful, remarkable people. God has blessed me indeed as my data base overflows with faith, hope and love.

Our love crosses over from heaven to earth, connecting a universal message of unity forever. I find great peace in the experiences I have had and I know when I am called home, my Mom and Dad will be with me to lead the way.

A short time ago, my friend Judy who you read about in chapters eight and nine lost her battle with lung cancer. At the young age of sixty-seven she remained committed to the God she served, trusting she would be blessed with a miraculous healing. Her cupboards lined with holistic treatments, her body withered from the effects of chemotherapy, were evidence of her struggle to live.

A week before her passing, Judy connected with her parents in the spirit world– who came to tell her it was time to journey home. She asked them for more time, but then humbly and with grace accepted their message that now was the time. Judy never allowed her shallow breathing or her pain, or even the inevitability of her death, to stop her from remaining faithful to her message of love. Maintaining her spirit of positivity she never gave way to anger or fear. Her miraculous healing that she fervently prayed for would take place in her transformation to new life.

Judy spent time with each family member and each friend, delivering messages of hope and faith through the very end. She instructed everyone, "No anger, only love." Judy's final words were, "I am ready." I believe she saw the light… the face of Christ and she peacefully journeyed into God's loving embrace.

Yes, I am awfully sad to experience the loss of such a great friend, a soul-mate, but I am forever grateful that our paths have crossed. It was an honor to call Judy my friend. Like our poem from Bethany, ordinary miracles take place daily through the bonds of love. We need to be open, accepting each channel of light. Judy taught me divine purpose and I am confident that our connection and love will transcend time and space, forever.

Someday when it's time, divine energy will lead us to our heavenly home where we will meet our God face-to-face, and we will reunite with those who have gone before us. But for now, we must do our best to live in the moment, enjoying each second of the gift of life. Our focus must remain on the journey, we must live in the light accepting our divine purpose…

To spread love and healing to all whom we meet!

Thank You

for reading Listen to the *Whisper*.

I invite you to share your thoughts and reactions
www.sandimatts.com

Bibliography

New Living Translation (NLT) Holy Bible. New Living Translation copyright© 1996, 2004, 2007, 2013 by Tyndale House Foundation. Used by permission of Tyndale House Publishers Inc., Carol Stream, Illinois 60188. All rights reserved. All Scripture quotations are retrieved at http://www.biblegateway.com

Bethany Retreat Center. "Homepage image Isaiah 2": Retrieved from http://www.bethanyretreatcenter.org

Crowell, Grace Noll. *God Hath Sent His Angel:* Compiled by Editors of Guideposts, 1993, p 38.

Emerson, Ralph Waldo. 'Middle School Journal': January 1992, Retrieved from http://quoteinvestigator.com/2014/06/19/new-path/

Haas, David, Composer. *We Will Rise Again:* Album You are Mine, 1995.

Lonestar. *Amazed:* Released March 1999, written by Green, Marv, Mayo Aimee and Lindsey, Chris.

Seuss, Dr. *Oh, the Places You'll Go!:* Random House, 1990.

Sisters of St. Joseph. *Spirit of Courage Award*: Retrieved at http://www.ssjerie.org/support-us/spirit-of-courage.php

Tuller, Grant Colfax . "The Weaver". b. 1869. Public Domain.

Venefica, Avia/ *Raven Symbolism and Symbolic Meaning of Ravens:* Retrieved at http://www.whats-your-sign.com/raven-symbolism.html

Made in the USA
Middletown, DE
14 August 2015